dining with the enemy

winnie nantongo

Copyright ©2023 by Winnie Nantongo.

All rights reserved. No part of this book may be used, reproduced, transmitted or stored in a retrieval system, or transmitted in any form or by any means (electronic, mechanical, photocopying, re-cording or otherwise), without permission in writing from the author of this book.

for Asha, Mark & you

with this ink

i aspire to write

everything

i left unsaid

contents

the mess we made 3

fucked my way out 71

the calm after 121

new beginnings 163

introduction

i tried fighting my demons
but their relentless grip
pushed me to surrender
so i chose to befriend them
and that nearly killed me
my fears and weaknesses
all got a hold of me
rendering me blind and captive
bringing anxiety and depression along
but writing unfolded me
to see their invisible strings
allowing me to break free
and gave me strength
to stop dining with the enemy

the mess we made

dining with the enemy

no glue in the world

can ever keep together

the pieces of me

that i broke

trying to reach

other people's expectations

winnie nantongo

in the quest

to please and align

i lost myself

a subtle decline

my heart

yearning for acceptance

yet my spirit is burning

lost in the void

dining with the enemy

been called loud

every time

i speak my mind

so i hold my tongue

because i care about

what they think

wish i meant it

every time

i said

i don't give a fuck

winnie nantongo

i don't remember

nights

when my heart

didn't ache

for their approval

dining with the enemy

could we just sleep in

because i don't want

to go out

then try to fit in

the voices in my head

whisper to me

every single night

winnie nantongo

i hate being alone
because that's when these little voices
in my head get the loudest
i'm tired of comparisons
tired of dissatisfaction
held hostage by anxiety
playing cards with my depression
always thinking i'm out of my mind
yet i'm doing just fine
maybe i'm over in my head
maybe i stopped seeing beauty
in the small little things
or maybe i stopped appreciating
the gift that life is

- *anxiety & depression*

dining with the enemy

hated the mirror for years

couldn't stand the look

on my face every time

my breast disappearing

in the palm of my hand

my collarbones are showing

i should cover them up

with a scarf

to everyone i'm making

a fashion statement

yet i'm concealing

my insecurities

you succeeded in making me
hate myself

winnie nantongo

and to think

all i ever wanted

was for someone

to love all the parts

that made me **me**

yet i couldn't

look twice at them

myself

dining with the enemy

how long is your natural hair

how tall are you

can you walk in heels

you can definitely make

a great model

all these

probably meant

to be compliments

but only reminded me

of why i hated myself

- my body never felt like mine

winnie nantongo

my biggest struggle in life
has always been
finding just one thing
that i can say
is my favorite thing
about myself

dining with the enemy

compliments are strange

in my ear

i struggle to believe

what i hear

you see a beauty

pure and bright

but shadows of doubt

still linger in sight

but i'll keep trying

won't give in

embracing the beauty

that lies within

- old habits die hard

winnie nantongo

i know i'm doing enough
by just being me
but why doesn't it
feel like it

dining with the enemy

i live in constant fear
of not measuring up
not being good enough
and on most days i feel like
i will never be good at this
like everyone else is

- *imposter syndrome*

there is this conversation

i keep having

with my inner child

i tell her i'm not enough

and she tells me

i'm more than enough

- self-doubt

dining with the enemy

you keep hurting me
every chance you get
and i keep coming back
to you
i should know better now
but i'm addicted to this
it's toxic love i know
but i can't walk away
i don't know anything else
but this
so i stay

winnie nantongo

when you don't know
what love feels like
you accept whatever
is offered to you

dining with the enemy

always tripping

right into the laps

of those who hurt me

because i'm a mess

and i hate being alone

so with a little bit of liquor

i will find my place

back in the same hands

that broke me once

- old patterns

winnie nantongo

i never learnt how to live

and be happy on my own

so i seek company

even in the same old places

get under a few bodies

for warmth

and to satisfy this hunger

of being touched and loved

to feel something

anything

dining with the enemy

one of my greatest mistakes
has been choosing people
who only choose me
because i'm the safer option

winnie nantongo

i knew

i deserved better

than people

who only wanted me

because they couldn't

have those

they desired the most

and yet

i still did let them

have me

dining with the enemy

i wasted a lot of time
clinging on to someone
whose efforts
could never match mine
but i was hoping that
maybe someday they will

winnie nantongo

it's not like

you ever made me

feel wanted

yet i still stayed

hoping one day

you'd wake up

and realize

you wanted me

the same way

that i wanted you

dining with the enemy

i guess
one of my greatest
mistakes in life
was believing that
being in a relationship
would heal me
i wish i knew then that
another person
couldn't fix me
i had to do the work
it was i who had
to take responsibility
for my own happiness

winnie nantongo

i still hate myself

every time i remember

how i thought i needed

to be around people

to be happy

i wanted them

to see me happy

so i pretended to be

even when my insides

were on fire

dining with the enemy

loving was okay

but i neglected

my heart

in the process

filled theirs with love

leaving mine empty

winnie nantongo

perhaps i needed
this heartbreak
to remind me
i have a heart
and it's deserving
of my love too

dining with the enemy

<u>no i don't hate you.</u>

i hope you find love
learn from our past
and treat her with kindness that lasts
hope she gets you mesmerized
makes your heart flutter
and your days brighter
but as i pick up these pieces
i hope your heart breaks too
hope you feel the pain and hurt
that you once caused me
may you know the betrayal and deceit
that left my heart shattered and numb
yes, i know it's bad
but part of me wants you to pay the cost
so as i wipe away the tears
i hope karma catches up to you in time

winnie nantongo

i prayed and hoped

for a forever with you

though deep down

i knew we'd

one day be through

despite my fear

of getting hurt again

i still risked it all for love

and two months in

i was yearning

to be free from your hold

dining with the enemy

why do i cling to a love

that was never mine

dream of a future that is gone

a fantasy that was never born

my heart aches for what will never be

but maybe it's time to break the hold

of a love that was never meant to unfold

winnie nantongo

growing up

i wish i'd known

that feelings

shouldn't be

concealed

and pretending

is not a charade

dining with the enemy

if only i could learn to hold

a love for myself, bright and bold

i wouldn't need to beg and plead

from those who only know

how to take and feed

winnie nantongo

wish i knew the art

of keeping love

for myself in heart

i'd cease to seek

from those who never impart

the love that they themselves

lack to start

if i could learn to love myself

i'd stop seeking love

from someone else

for in my heart

i'd have enough wealth

to sustain me

through life's every delph

dining with the enemy

you say it's the last time

same words you say every time

i know i should walk away

yet i stay

hoping someday

our love will endure

flee the pain

or confront it

find release

or face its remorse

should i unlove you

or lose myself

walk away

or risk breaking my heart

because staying means

losing my mind

- *crossroads*

dining with the enemy

i knew my feelings

for you were

a suffocating obsession

not a blissful infatuation

yet i still loved how it felt

for once

i could feel something **again**

and i wasn't willing

to let that go

winnie nantongo

we were so different

and yet our demons

were not so dissimilar

dining with the enemy

with a frozen heart

and weary eyes

i mask the pain

with a forced grin

and lay in your arms

i wonder if you can tell

from the tar on my lips

or you're thinking

about someone else

even as we kiss

winnie nantongo

i knew about the women
he had met before me
the wild nights
filled with liquor
and cigarettes
sex with strangers
and violence
his gambling addiction
he told me about that too
but i wasn't here to save him
and he knew that too
at least he would be easy
to get over
so i chose him
not like i deserved any better
or maybe i just didn't care
i was lost too

dining with the enemy

for how long
do i have to hold onto the hope
that time will eventually heal
the parts of me
you caused pain

for how long
do i have to hold onto the hope
that one day these memories of you
will stop bringing tears
to my eyes

i hoped for peace and joy
yet all you caused me
was pain and regret
memories of you have turned
into nightmares that haunt me

winnie nantongo

with shattered pieces

my heart still yearns

for love's sweet bliss

so it foolishly falls

time and again

ignoring the lessons

of the heartache

and finds itself in hurt

once more

a pattern it cannot resist

dining with the enemy

to my favorite ex:

i was your first love

and yet i left you broken

you gave me a special part of you

and i vowed to treasure it forever

but i lied

i didn't deserve your heart

for me forever was a moment

i'm sorry you didn't deserve

to be responsible for kissing away

the scars that were caused by those

who came before you

i will always remember you

as the one

who loved me fearlessly

even though i wasn't worth it

winnie nantongo

remember:

love cannot flourish when it finds
comfort in complacency—wish i knew this earlier

dining with the enemy

i hate to think

you moved on

that quickly

after you embedded

your touch into

the fabric of my skin

was i that easy

to forget

winnie nantongo

may be i hold onto

the memories

of you and me

because it's what

remains of

what once was

dining with the enemy

you kept pushing me away
and yet i kept coming back
fighting for a place in your heart
desperate to be desired
and loved by you

self-blame.

it's not your fault that i made myself yours when i knew you were never truly mine, and it's not your fault that i still hope one day you will come to me yet i pushed you to find a home in yourself.

dining with the enemy

why did you make me fall
when you knew
you couldn't catch me
you made me feel things
you knew you didn't feel

i already know how this ends
with my heart in pieces

winnie nantongo

you know what's pathetic

the fact that i always

found an excuse

for your toxic behavior

dining with the enemy

all the scars

that i thought were fading

resurfaced

and every time you called

your voice dug in deeper

revealing the old wounds

winnie nantongo

i knew
a love like this
would leave
a permanent scar
but i couldn't stop myself
from wanting you
even when i knew
you didn't feel
the same way that i did
i still hoped

dining with the enemy

every memory

of a moment

i took for granted

still lingers

hunting me

reminding me

of what i had

but didn't keep

winnie nantongo

i knew some connections are not meant to last
and some people are not meant to stay
yet i still chose to build a home in you

dining with the enemy

to my ex best friend:

oh how you spoke

with such ease

words flowing

like a gentle breeze

made promises so grand

a poet's tongue you had

crafting verses

like sunlight on petals clad

i believed them all

without any fight

but your empty words

and hollow promises

were like castles

built on shifting sand

fading into echoes

slipping through my hand

winnie nantongo

i yearned for your promises

to bloom and unfold

to finally witness the sincerity

your words had foretold

but alas

the distance between

your words and actions

remained

dining with the enemy

i fell in love

with a broken man

who tasted like glass

and smelled like dust

tried to fix him

but he was so dry

he sucked me in

and left me empty

on skins and bones

winnie nantongo

i have been a people pleaser my entire life and that came at a high price. i lost touch with my own authenticity and forgot who i truly was. found myself saying yes to things that didn't align with my values, and as a result, i formed connections with people who were ultimately bad for my well-being and my soul.

dining with the enemy

sleepless nights

holding my breath

i slowly count down

from ten to zero

like the night before

i cry myself to sleep

and wake up exhausted

from the nightmares

i'm not suicidal

but lately my heart

feels too heavy

it's becoming hard

to carry all

these emotions

winnie nantongo

i guess

i found it easier

to blame alcohol

for the same mistakes

i would still make sober

some nights i lay down to sleep with fears of not waking up when morning comes and no one finds out until it's like a day or two since no one ever checks up on me. what troubles me even more is that these concerns arise despite being in good health. i have heard stories of those who go to sleep and never open their eyes again. i wonder if they can feel themselves taking their last breath, if it's a painful or peaceful death.

winnie nantongo

when life bids goodbye

do dreams gently fade

or anguish prevails

in a restless grave

dining with the enemy

today i woke up in pain
just like yesterday
feeling lost and insane
with thoughts of ways
i could meet my end
whispers of sweet release
echoing through my brain
maybe the end
will be a beautiful start
yet something holds me back
thoughts of those i love
whose lives would forever be low
so i'm holding on, clinging to hope
and fighting to find a way to cope

- suicidal thoughts

the fear of the unknown

is too great to ignore

what lies on the other end

is a mystery i cannot explore

but i find peace

at the thought

of those i hold dear

whose love is so clear

winnie nantongo

in the shadows i hide
scared of the world outside
i keep my true self away
a weight too heavy to bear
for i feel the hatred in their words
and it only adds to my fears
the hate that surrounds
is a constant weight that grounds
my existence is a constant debate
an easy target for their rage
my rights in constant grief
equality is a distant dream
my life on the line
my soul is tormented
and my mind is racing
anxiety hunting my spaces
afraid to speak or truly live
homophobia's venom is a bitter pill

dining with the enemy

but for in my heart a fire burns bright
a passion for love your sad soul can't feel
so to you who cannot understand
who judge me by the lies they've planned
i say this with strength and poise
i am who i am, with love, in my heart
but if your intention was to crush my spirit
you almost succeeded

- the anti-homosexuality bill 2023

winnie nantongo

i haven't been

to church this year

i don't blame God

for the choices

i've made

but if it's wrong

why does it feel

so right

a journey

i must tread alone

to find where faith

and truth align

fucked my way out

dining with the enemy

recently i realized

the devil is in my mind

and it's cutting me

like a knife

but yet again

i sharpen its blades

by letting in

negative thoughts

until i bleed

and fall to my knees

but lord today i pray

save me

i can't do this on my own

winnie nantongo

though the devil's whispers

may persist

with unwavering strength

i aspire to rise above

each star

a testament to a story born

a new chapter.

somethings break you

only to rebuild you

some people leave you

only to make room for new ones

and so do chapters close

just for a new one to begin

don't water yourself down

all you need is faith

trust the timing

everything happens for a reason

and things change for the better

winnie nantongo

the thing

about having faith

is that even as it hurts

you hope

even as you cry

you pray

dining with the enemy

i'm ready to meet the new version
of myself once i heal from all this
tragic mess i have been through

winnie nantongo

for once in my life

i want to do what's right

for my soul

i want to choose me

be gentle with myself

and love myself a little more

dining with the enemy

my greatest pain

was also my most

needed reminder

not everything is worth

fighting for

winnie nantongo

listen;

> not everyone can be saved
> be okay with walking away
> if that's what it takes for you
> to protect your mental health

dining with the enemy

i feel like

all my heartaches

came from trying so hard

to fill the void

with something that

could only be discovered

from within

- love

winnie nantongo

finding love

with another

won't heal you

if you haven't found it

within yourself yet

dining with the enemy

i'm learning to love
all the parts of me
that made me
a colorful mess
i once was

the parts of me
that made me
hate my name

the parts of me
that made me
wish i could crawl out
of this skin

winnie nantongo

even at my worst

i hope to never feel

like i'm not enough

- *a prayer*

dining with the enemy

chasing after relationships

is like chasing stars

it has gotten me closer

to nowhere

winnie nantongo

you don't have

to chase things

when you are naturally

in tune and aligned

with them

dining with the enemy

i hold myself accountable
for giving those that hurt me
access to my space again
choosing them the first time
was okay
but the second and third time
was out of habit
i did this to myself

- *i'm not a victim*

winnie nantongo

i never chose pain

because i thought i deserved it

but it's just that my silly heart

was being so hopeful

that maybe

at some point

it would all make sense

that maybe

eventually it would all be worth it

and maybe things didn't turn out

the way i expected

but at least all that hurt

made me the person

that i am today

dining with the enemy

you don't have to be

okay with everything

nor let yourself

be taken for a fall

just because you're scared

of losing them

your worth should never

be overlooked

nor your boundaries

ever be mistook

winnie nantongo

to whom this may concern;

when toxicity obscures your sight
resist the urge to cling so tight
to souls that offer naught but pain
you deserve to be treated with respect
never sacrifice your dignity or pride
just to keep someone by your side
walk away and let their darkness
not dim your light

dining with the enemy

sometimes

on the journey of moving on

the pain we once felt lingers on and on

relentlessly haunting our every thought

but with each passing day

and every tear shed

we slowly begin to release the dread

until finally

the pain no longer remains

and we can move on

without any strains

winnie nantongo

a gentle reminder:

moving on from someone who once meant everything to you doesn't happen overnight. it's a process that requires time, patience, and unwavering strength. but although the journey can be a long and difficult one, you eventually reach a stage where all the heartache that once plagued you fades into a distant memory.

dining with the enemy

i yearn to learn

to love myself

just as deeply and true

as the love i had for you

to see myself with grace

that i once saw in you

and hold my heart

in gentle hands

the way i held yours

winnie nantongo

i recognize that the love i seek must originate from within. it is a commitment to acceptance, forgiveness, and kindness, woven delicately into the very essence of my being. through mindful introspection, i hope to unravel the layers of self-doubt and criticism, replacing them with a beautiful blend of self-worth and gratitude.

dining with the enemy

i found my

greatest superpower

when i finally

accepted the truth

that you weren't mine

to have

yes, it did hurt at first

but i summoned

my strength

and forged

a new path forward

and though i still

think about you

sometimes

it's all love

winnie nantongo

i hope happiness find you
wherever you roam
and joy paint vibrant hues
upon your soul
i hope you don't
let another one go
just because your heart
is scared of the good ones

- to the one i used to know

dining with the enemy

i wish someone told me

i didn't have to change myself

to been seen or heard

i wish i knew that i didn't have

to be a certain way

to be understood

only if i'd known earlier

that you can't be for everyone

- different is attractive

winnie nantongo

in a world consumed by conformity, the pressure to change oneself to fit societal molds looms heavily. but here's a truth we often forget: you don't have to alter your essence to gain acceptance. you can never be universally appealing, so instead, embrace your true self and allow others to appreciate and love you just the way you are. that in itself is a remarkable gift.

dining with the enemy

i used to give

my all

then wondered

why i always

felt empty

winnie nantongo

you should never pour

all your energy and attention

into nurturing

and supporting others

leaving no room

for your own needs

and self-care

or else you will

feel drained and depleted

dining with the enemy

may this find its way to your heart
once the shaper of my identity
may it unveil the struggles and pain
i endured within your walls
realize how your words and judgments
became chains that confined my spirit
making me hate the person i was
may others escape your rigid expectations
may they never sacrifice authenticity
for acceptance
nor wander through life clouded by doubt
and self-criticism
your relentless scrutiny left deep scars
of self-doubt
but i hope others realize sooner that
their worth cannot be defined
by your standards
or confined within the boundaries you impose

winnie nantongo

dear society

your words

warped around me

cracked my every bone

and left me crippled

dining with the enemy

all i ever prayed for

was a forever with you

and even when it hurt

i hoped it would

eventually stop

because we have been

told to be patient

trust in time

and i did

just to end up

sucked and dry

winnie nantongo

only now

do i realize

that no amount

of time or patience

could have saved us

dining with the enemy

deep within

i always knew my worth

yet strangely

i was dying to hear it

from someone else

- *thirst for validation*

winnie nantongo

i was chained

to other's approval

flashing my art

is it good

i'd ask

my heart aching

for applause

from strangers

seeking solace

in their praises

yet i couldn't take it

if they said anything

that didn't appease

my sensitive ears

dining with the enemy

if only i had loved

myself a little more

embraced my flaws

and believed i'm worthy

instead i dwelled

on my imperfections

and ignored my strengths

losing sight of my beauty

yet self-love is where it all begins

winnie nantongo

<u>regrets.</u>

i wish i had learned to prioritize myself earlier. if only i had known that i don't have to shoulder the responsibility of fixing everyone around me.

dining with the enemy

there has always been

that feeling

in the back of my mind

somehow i have always

known that

you don't mean

every word you say

and yet i have always

looked for an excuse

as to why you treat me

the way you do

winnie nantongo

if your heart is doubting it, it sure isn't it. someone who truly wants you will go above and beyond to make you feel it. if they aren't making an effort take that as a sign that they aren't interested regardless of what they tell you.

- *actions will always reflect what they hide in their words.*

dining with the enemy

i don't want to go another day

thinking about whether

i should trust you or play you

because you see,

i can't let you slip away either

the first, and the second

weren't so good to me

not that the recent one

was any different

but then you seem like

a good one

and for once i want

to ignore my mind

and listen to my heart

but it hasn't proven itself

reliable when it comes to such

winnie nantongo

unhealed trauma
will make you think
every lover you meet
is up to something

dining with the enemy

sometimes

all it takes to find peace

is to remove some people

some habits

or even some food

from your life

important:

>just because someone is your family
>
>doesn't mean
>
>you have to keep them around
>
>if they are toxic or abusive.
>
>don't let people guilt you.

dining with the enemy

i can't believe all it took

for me to finally surmount

was putting my guns down

and now my serenity thrives

in the same space

where my pride once bred chaos

winnie nantongo

i'm slowly learning that i don't have to react to every single thing in order to maintain control over situations that are beyond me. that it okay to accept defeat at times, and that there is strength in allowing certain things to simply exist as they are.

dining with the enemy

i wish i had learnt

at a younger age

how peaceful it is

to pour warmth

into spaces

and people

that feel like home

winnie nantongo

sometimes i wonder

do people like you

ever miss people

like me

who were once kind

and lovely to you

do you ever think

about us

and beat yourself up

for playing us

the way you did

dining with the enemy

it felt like the end

as if my world

was coming to a stop

took me forever

to realize how freeing

living without the thought

of waking up to your barrage

of 20 angry texts

just because i couldn't

answer your phone call

at 2am

and then

i met her

winnie nantongo

sometimes

in order to receive

what you truly deserve

you must first release

the things that drain you

the calm after

dining with the enemy

i hope one day

i get to feel

how it feels

to be loved right

but until then

i will be here loving myself

the way i deserve to be loved

winnie nantongo

there is a serene strength in cherishing oneself welcoming the gentle whispers of self-worth. a steadfast essence flourishes, proclaiming that until the day love arrives in its fullest form, the heart shall remain a sanctuary of self – love, a place where deserving affection takes root and blossoms into a radiant force.

dining with the enemy

i'm always looking

for the best in people

although most times

it breaks me

i'm always glad

that i tried

winnie nantongo

i don't wish

to unmeet anyone

because i know

there was definitely

a lesson in every

connection

dining with the enemy

i have come to learn

that some people

are only moments

that are meant

to stay in our past

it doesn't matter how much

we love them or even try

to make it work

we will always remember

and cherish them

but won't have them again

and that's why

you can't change

what was bound

to happen

winnie nantongo

some connections

are not meant to last

however much we

would want them to

dining with the enemy

the people i have

loved the most

have painfully

broken me

yet i still move on

and love again

winnie nantongo

the scars might

be permanent

but the pain

won't last forever

don't be afraid

to let yourself fall

dining with the enemy

as life takes us

in different directions

i promise to not hold on to

the sting of a goodbye

but to cherish

the moments with you

that brought me joy

and comfort

- farewell my love

winnie nantongo

to love this deeply

and not be loved

in return

is the worst feeling

yet the one lesson

i needed the most

dining with the enemy

i was never

colorblind

to the red flags

i just hoped

i was wrong

winnie nantongo

i pray

the next time

i fall

i don't do it

blindly

dining with the enemy

thank the universe

i finally realized

that loving you

was never

reason enough

for you to deserve me

winnie nantongo

all it took

was losing myself

for me to finally realize

that i too deserve

the same love that i give

and not the bare minimum

they gave in return

dining with the enemy

time and

knowledge

will change

your truths

winnie nantongo

people eventually

reveal themselves

its only

a matter

of time

dining with the enemy

the healing journey

can be tumultuous

yet amidst the shadows

lies a stunning radiance

so trust its distinct phases

even when it seems

uncomfortable

winnie nantongo

some people

are going to drain you

and leave you empty

empty of self-love

and peace of mind

be brave enough

to walk away

the journey to self-love

involves discovering yourself

accepting yourself

and embracing who you are

there are no shortcuts

winnie nantongo

i have mastered the art of self-love and i think there is totally nothing that can ever make me feel smaller than i already am.

dear me;

please don't let

the heartbreak

turn you into

a stranger

i'm still afraid

of the unknown

winnie nantongo

i know one day

mentioning your name

will bring a smile to my face

instead of this twinge of pain

- *the healing power of time*

dining with the enemy

had i known

choosing myself

was all i had to do

to move on from you

i would've broken

my toe running to myself

winnie nantongo

if it takes

losing myself

loving you

i don't want it

dining with the enemy

the problem was never
about making peace
with my sadness
or housing it in these
strong beautiful walls
the problem started when
i got comfortable living
in this new lonely house
that i almost chose to stay

winnie nantongo

depression is a dirty bitch, capable of distorting your perceptions and leaving you unsure of what exactly feels amiss. that restless adversary can make you sad out of the blue and make you isolate from things that would make you feel yellow. with hard work, eventually, you reach a point where you must stop finding excuses to be sad or so you tell yourself. yet, just when you believe you've made progress, that insidious foe makes a comeback and hits you hard, pushing you further back than the strides you diligently made.

dining with the enemy

dear you;

i want you to know that mistakes are an essential aspect of personal growth and healing. so, don't let them discourage you, but instead embrace them as opportunities to learn and improve.

winnie nantongo

19.04.2023

i haven't been myself in a long time. maybe it has something to do with age, space, and all these new beautiful addictions. but i really hope it has something to do with the fact that i'm growing, learning, and unlearning everything i was taught to believe growing up.

dining with the enemy

i feel too much sometimes

and when i love

it's with my whole soul

and i try to heal everyone i love

because i feel everything they feel

so i have felt more heartaches

than my own

winnie nantongo

and for how much

i have grown

i would live it all again

dining with the enemy

it took me a while
to find a safe haven
where i could heal
and never look back

a while to realize
that all my past choices
were not always made
from a place of kindness
but rather as a response
to past traumas

it took me a while
to finally come
back to myself

winnie nantongo

the real flex is in healing yourself
such that you don't have to match low vibe energy
to meet the mark to fit in.
lowering your standards to connect with others
is unhealed trauma response.

dining with the enemy

they will notice

and envy your success

but not how much work

you've put in

to go from the bottom up

that's their problem

be proud of the person

that you have become

you deserve it

winnie nantongo

sweat, tears, and countless hours—these are hidden treasures, manifestations of your incredible power. the sacrifices you've made, the lessons you've learned, they demonstrate the strength within, battles you've fought. with unwavering pride, let your soul roam free. from the depths you rose, an inspiration for all.

dining with the enemy

my healing journey

started with

accepting that

i wasn't

the best version

of myself

that i believed

i could be

winnie nantongo

when the world came

crumbling down

my spirits fell

exposing all my flaws

but a seed of hope within

yearned for growth

for a brand new start

but for healing blooms

only when we acknowledge

our imperfections

and learn to accept

every part that shapes us

into who we truly are

dining with the enemy

living your truth

is so healing

never hide parts

of you because

you are scared

of other people's

judgments

winnie nantongo

not to fear for love is a growth for the soul, to know that there are no limitations or taboos to develop feelings for someone, regardless of genitalia, only to feel and not condemn oneself. enjoy life as a nest of opportunities.

dining with the enemy

at some point

you will have to learn

to let go

of what does not

want to stay

winnie nantongo

if they want to leave

trust me they will

it doesn't matter

what you say or do

and i learned that

the hard way

new beginnings

dining with the enemy

at last

i've turned the last chapter

of our tale

and started crafting

my own rhyme

where i'm no longer bound

to your plot

so farewell to that character

trapped in a narrative

of your making

i'm now an author

of a story

that's uniquely my own

winnie nantongo

here i stand

both author and muse

creating a universe

in vivid hues

my own soul's cruise

dining with the enemy

saw you

with someone else

and it didn't hurt

this time

congratulations to me

winnie nantongo

i guess i found it
hard to move on
from you
because i thought
you might start loving me
just when i have stopped
loving you

dining with the enemy

i hope you find

someone who

will not only

fall for the hope

in your eyes

but also

the chaos

in your mind

winnie nantongo

one day;

i hope you meet someone who truly cares for you and brings out the best in you, not highlight your flaws and weaknesses but someone who inspires you and focuses on your strengths, and claps for you as you turn into the confident and amazing person you have always been meant to be.

dining with the enemy

be okay with

cutting off people

who repeatedly try

to cross your boundaries

winnie nantongo

i hope you understand that preserving your peace and well-being by distancing from toxic individuals is not a sign of harshness, but of self-care.

dining with the enemy

life has taught me

that sometimes

all you need

is rest

rest your mind

and listen

to your silence

winnie nantongo

i've strived too hard for happiness to let the negative energy diminish it. my time and energy are valuable and i refuse to expend them on negativity.

dining with the enemy

i'm now fighting demons
that weren't mine to own
my brain is a battlefield
and as i sing sorrow's tune
these unbidden guests dance
wreaking havoc within my chest
i try to play a hopeful melody
but their haunting echoes
claiming space in my troubled mind

winnie nantongo

amidst the chaos and the strife
i hope you find a calm and peaceful life
may you discover within yourself
a soothing haven, a place of help
even in times of trouble
may you find inner strength and might
in moments when the world is loud
may you find peace in the quiet shroud
i hope you hold onto hope and grace
and find comfort in a warm embrace

dining with the enemy

be around people

who want more for you

not from you

winnie nantongo

be mindful that even those
who emit the most alluring scent
can still be toxic to your well-being

dining with the enemy

we met at a time

when my hurt

was too heavy to carry

i now understand

why you had to walk away

you had to save yourself

loving me meant losing yourself

winnie nantongo

as you take care of others

don't forget

to take care of yourself

you're as important

dining with the enemy

hurt can be expressed
without fear of blame
emotions need to be processed
to heal and overcome the pain

winnie nantongo

not every wrong will receive an apology and not every emotion will be acknowledged. but always keep it in mind that your feelings are valid, even when others remain ignorant to the hurt they've caused you.

dining with the enemy

the greatest lovers

often encounter

the harshest realities of love

may your spirit never tire

and your heart never lose its fire

winnie nantongo

a reminder:

you deserve someone who embraces your authentic self and encourages personal growth. one who seeks not to fill a void, but to enhance the completeness you already possess. you deserve a love that celebrates your worth.

dining with the enemy

dear god,

if i ever love again

please let it be

from a healed place

winnie nantongo

healing is personal

don't do it

for anyone else

but yourself

dining with the enemy

don't you ever let them

make you doubt

who you are

it's only you

who truly knows you

winnie nantongo

i have a good heart
and if you lost me
that's on you

dining with the enemy

don't you ever be afraid
to take a step back
from people whose darkness is so full
that it's ever threatening
to invade your light

winnie nantongo

your energy

should stay

exclusive

not everyone

deserves it

dining with the enemy

it's quite amusing how i constantly struggled to let go of toxic people in my life, even though i knew it would bring me peace. yet now, it's the one thing i have mastered so well. honestly, making the decision to break free from their grasp isn't easy, but the moment you do and finally get to experience the joy it brings, you will realize how much you have been missing out on just to keep their memory alive.

winnie nantongo

may you finally

have the mental strength

to finally let go

of people and situations

that only cause you pain

may you finally

get to experience

the happiness

that comes with

walking away

dining with the enemy

but darling

cease the chase

the competition

should be between

you and your past self

not you versus them

winnie nantongo

i would ask you
to lend me an ear
for this heartfelt plea
but it's your eyes i need
for a reminder
to set your own self free

darling,
don't focus on what
everyone else
is doing
you have your own mission
stick to it
gyenva tugamba;
  "omukisa gw'embwa
teguyisa mbuzi mu malagala"
ate era "tobuukira munno
wabuukidde"

navigating adulthood presents a formidable challenge as it demands unwavering perseverance. regardless of the emotional state or circumstances you find yourself in, you've got to keep pushing forward because life continues its course and so should you.

winnie nantongo

in the face of trials

when hope seems lost

and shadows linger

casting a doubt

i hope resilience

becomes

your warrior song

i refuse to resolve every little disagreement. i'm content with being misunderstood. i won't keep repeating myself for those who lack the inclination to listen. i've come to accept the importance of protecting my energy.

winnie nantongo

while it may be tempting to confront certain issues, there are times when it's better to leave them unaddressed. frankly, not everything is worth the effort, so it's important to choose your battles wisely and preserve your inner peace.

dining with the enemy

i hope

in all the next chapters

of my life

i'm kinder to myself

winnie nantongo

and the best part

of all this

is that now

i know myself enough

to know that

there are still parts of me

that i'm yet to discover

also by winnie nantongo

the lover and her human

about the author

winnie nantongo is a writer. author. poet. and creative. in 2021, she wrote and self-published her first poetry collection *the lover and her human*. now here comes a prose and poetry collection *dining with the enemy*. winnie's work centers around love, growth, healing, inspiration, activism and affirmations.

Made in the USA
Middletown, DE
26 April 2025